When Birds Change Their Feathers

This Is a Let's-Read-and-Find-Out Science Book®

When Birds Change Their Feathers

by Roma Gans   Illustrated by Felicia Bond

Thomas Y. Crowell   New York

Other *Let's-Read-and-Find-Out Science Books*® You Will Enjoy

Shooting Stars • A Drop of Blood • My Five Senses • What Happened to the Dinosaurs? • Switch On, Switch Off • Ducks Don't Get Wet • Feel the Wind • The Skeleton Inside You • Digging Up Dinosaurs • Tornado Alert • The Sun: Our Nearest Star • The Beginning of the Earth • Eclipse • Dinosaur Bones • Glaciers • Snakes Are Hunters • Danger—Icebergs! • Comets • Evolution • Rockets and Satellites • The Planets in Our Solar System • The Moon Seems to Change • Ant Cities • Get Ready for Robots! • Gravity is a Mystery • Snow Is Falling • Journey into a Black Hole • What Makes Day and Night • Air is All Around You • Turtle Talk • What the Moon Is Like • Hurricane Watch • Sunshine Makes the Seasons • My Visit to the Dinosaurs • The BASIC Book • Bits and Bytes • Germs Make Me Sick! • Flash, Crash, Rumble, and Roll • Volcanoes • Dinosaurs Are Different • What Happens to a Hamburger • Meet the Computer • How to Talk to Your Computer • Rock Collecting • Is There Life in Outer Space? • All Kinds of Feet • Flying Giants of Long Ago • Rain and Hail • Why I Cough, Sneeze, Shiver, Hiccup & Yawn • You Can't Make a Move Without Your Muscles • The Sky Is Full of Stars • No Measles, No Mumps for Me

The *Let's-Read-and-Find-Out Science Book* series was originated by Dr. Franklyn M. Branley, Astronomer Emeritus and former Chairman of the American Museum-Hayden Planetarium, and was formerly co-edited by him and Dr. Roma Gans, Professor Emeritus of Childhood Education, Teachers College, Columbia University. For a complete catalog of Let's-Read-and-Find-Out Science Books, write to Thomas Y. Crowell Junior Books, Harper & Row, Publishers, Inc., 10 East 53rd Street, New York, NY 10022.
Let's-Read-and-Find-Out Science Book is a registered trademark of Harper & Row, Publishers, Inc.

Library of Congress Cataloging in Publication Data

Gans, Roma, 1894–
When birds change their feathers.
(Let's-read-and-find-out science books)
   SUMMARY: Describes how and why animals shed their feathers, hair, shells, etc., with emphasis on the molting of birds.
   1. Birds—Physiology—Juvenile literature. 2. Molting—Juvenile literature. [1. Molting. 2. Birds]
I. Bond, Felicia. II. Title.
QL698.G27   598.2'1'858   78-20627
ISBN 0-690-03947-6
ISBN 0-690-03948-4 lib. bdg.

When Birds Change Their Feathers

Dogs shed hair in warm weather. This makes their coats thinner and cooler. Horses get thinner coats, too, and so do cats. When cold weather comes, they grow thicker coats.

The snake rubs its nose against a tree trunk or a rock until its skin breaks away. Then the snake slides out of the old skin. It takes a snake only fifteen minutes to do this.

As a snake grows, the old skin gets too tight for it. The snake wriggles and squirms and slides right out of its skin. The old skin is left behind. Often it is all in one piece.

Lobsters and crabs outgrow their shells.
They leave their hard shells. They grow new
ones that at first are softer than the old ones.

When an animal sheds its outer covering, it is
molting. Many animals molt, and you do, too. You
change your skin. You don't lose all of it at once.
When you take a bath, you rub off some of it. You
shed part of your skin.

Animals like dogs and cats and horses shed their hair and get thinner coats. Animals like snakes and lobsters grow too big for their skins. So they get new ones. The old skin doesn't fit anymore.

You and I shed our skin because the old
skin is worn-out. That's what birds do, too. They
shed their old worn-out feathers.

7

In winter and spring, blue jays flit from tree to tree. Their feathers are shiny.

In late summer, the blue jays look ragged around their necks. They have lost some of their feathers. The blue jays are molting. This means they are losing their old feathers and getting new ones. After several weeks, all their old feathers will be gone. The blue jay's new feathers will be smooth and shiny.

Late summer

Several weeks later

SPRING

bright and shiny

SUMMER

worn and ragged

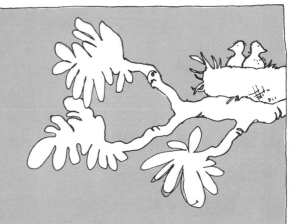

Woodpeckers also lose their feathers. First, they lose a few tail feathers. The tail feathers are strong. Woodpeckers use them to push against trees when they climb. In spring the feathers are bright and shiny. Later in summer, they look worn and ragged. When the feathers fall out, woodpeckers have stubby tails until new feathers grow.

All birds molt—even ducks and chickens and turkeys. But they may molt at different times. Some birds, like the blue jays, molt only once a year, right after their young have left the nest. Others, like the goldfinch, molt twice a year. They molt for the first time in spring, even before they build their nests. They molt the second time in late summer.

BLUE JAY

once a year

GOLDFINCH

twice a year

Most birds drop their
feathers one by one.
Feather after feather, they
change their whole coats.

14

Only a few birds, like the penguin, change all their feathers at once. The new feathers push out the old ones. The penguin pulls them off. The new feathers are underneath, so a penguin is never naked.

No bird ever looks naked while molting.

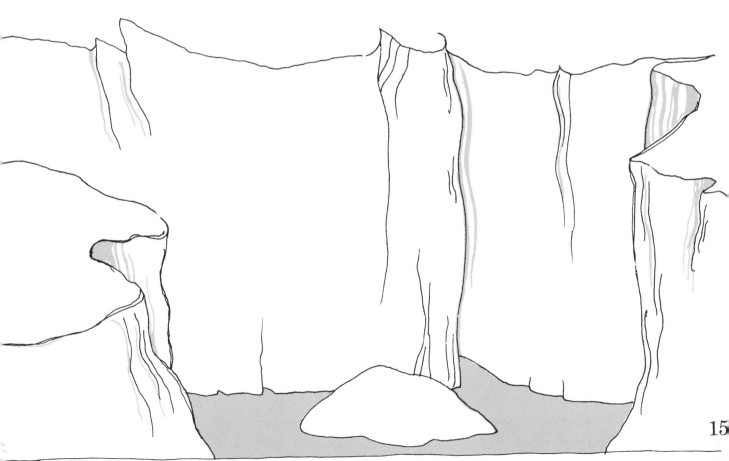

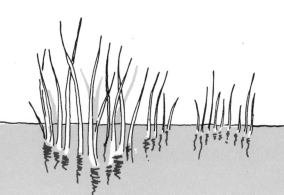

Ducks and geese lose all their big wing
feathers at one time. They cannot fly without
these feathers. But they can swim and get their
food from lakes and rivers. In a few weeks,
when their new wing feathers have grown, they
will fly again.

When birds hatch, they have no feathers, just soft fuzz. This is their baby blanket. Soon feathers take the place of the fuzz. Each feather comes out of a very small hole or pit in the skin. You can see the pits in a chicken's skin before it is fried or roasted.

Blood and food go into each new feather to
make it grow. As soon as the feather is
full-grown, no more blood and food go into it.

one day old

one week old

two weeks old

Feathers grow fast.
Baby sparrows have a full
coat in only two weeks.

SPARROW

Once the big wing and tail feathers
are grown, the bird is ready to fly.

The big wing and tail feathers are very strong. They are called flight feathers. Each bird has only a few of them. Many birds have only nine flight feathers in their wings.

They may have only ten or twelve flight feathers in their tails.

The wind can bend these feathers, but the feathers will not break. If by accident a feather does break, it does not hurt the bird. Later a new feather will grow from the same pit.

Birds have hundreds and hundreds of
feathers, if you count all the feathers, both the
big ones and the small ones. Even the tiny,
ruby-throated hummingbird has over nine
hundred. The goldfinch has over two thousand
in winter, but fewer in summer.

24

Many birds have more feathers in winter than in summer. They need a winter coat to keep warm.

Underneath the big wing and tail feathers, birds have many smaller feathers. They are called contour feathers. Hundreds of them cover their bodies.

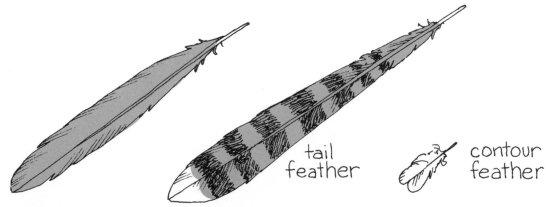

wing feather

tail feather

contour feather

BLUE JAY

The contour feathers make birds look smooth and shiny.

Under the contour feathers are hundreds of
even smaller feathers. When a bird puffs these
out, air is trapped among the feathers. This
makes the bird look larger. Birds do this in cold
weather. The trapped air keeps them warm.

When birds molt, they lose all their feathers, the large feathers and the small ones. It takes a purple finch ten weeks to finish molting. Other birds take even longer. Some birds molt very fast. The penguin is one of the fastest. It molts all at once.

SLOW
Purple Finch: ten weeks

FAST
Penguin: all at once

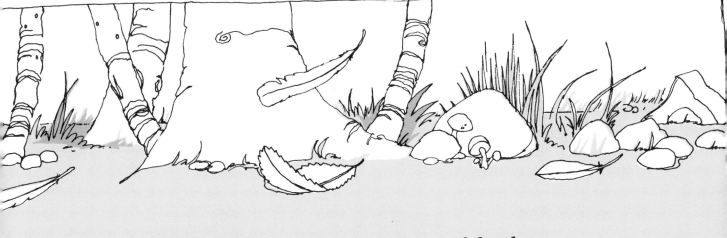

What happens to the millions of feathers
that fall?

Feathers are very light. The wind blows
them from place to place. They mix with leaves
and soil and rot away. If you look, you can find
bird feathers in the grass, or you might see
them caught on the branches of shrubs.

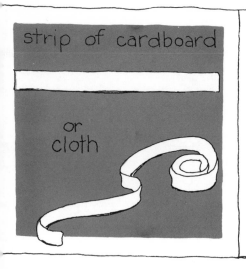
strip of cardboard or cloth

glue

GOO GLUE

feathers

You may want to collect feathers. You could fasten them to a strip of cloth or cardboard to make an Indian headband.

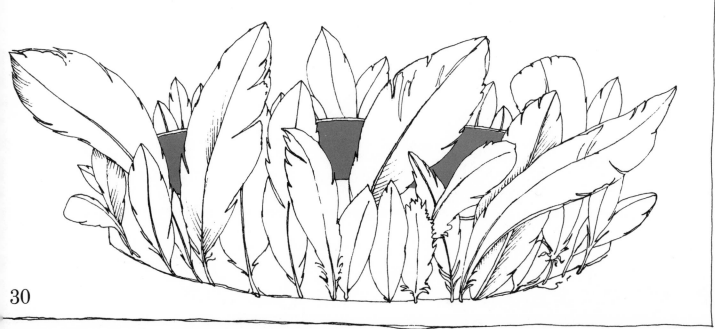

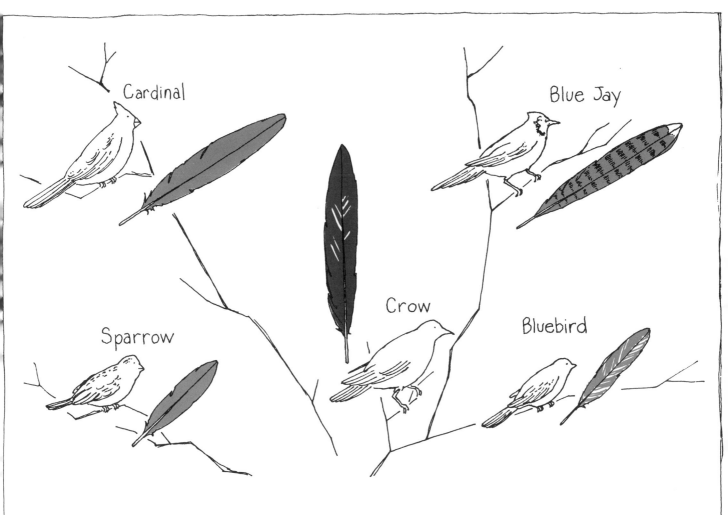

You may find red feathers from the
cardinal, blue and white ones from the blue jay,
and shiny black ones from the crow. Some of
your feathers may be large, some small. You'll
have feathers from many different kinds of birds.

You'll be wearing the birds' old feathers while they are flying about in their new ones.

About the Author

Roma Gans has called children "enlightened, excited citizens." She believes in the fundamental theory that children are eager to learn and will whet their own intellectual curiosity if they have stimulating teachers and books. She herself is the author of a number of books in the Let's-Read-and-Find-Out series.

Dr. Gans received her B.S. from Columbia Teachers College and her Ph.D. from Columbia University. She began her work in the education field in the public schools of the Middle West as a teacher, supervisor, and assistant superintendent of schools. She is Professor Emeritus of Childhood Education at Teachers College, Columbia University, and lectures extensively throughout the United States and Canada.

Dr. Gans lives in West Redding, Connecticut, on eleven acres of land, where she enjoys watching and feeding many different kinds of birds.

About the Illustrator

Felicia Bond was born in Japan, grew up in New York and Texas, and was graduated from the University of Texas with a Bachelor of Fine Arts degree. Her botanical illustrations have appeared in various academic journals as well as in science text books. This is the first book for children she has illustrated. Ms. Bond now lives in Texas.